Devoted

Aby Young

Presentation by *BookLeaf Publishing*

Web: www.bookleafpub.com

E-mail: info@bookleafpub.com

ISBN: 9789358368994

First edition 2023

DEDICATION

A teacher who took the time to listen. The only thing I ever needed was for someone to show me my life mattered. That I had purpose. You did that. I will forever be grateful.

ACKNOWLEDGEMENT

My amazing children, Andrew, Kira and Paige. You are the light of my world.

PREFACE

Writing has always been my release. Normally I would only write when I was sad, lonely or lost someone. Now I write because I enjoy it. I do still pour my pain out on paper at times, but now I try to inspire and relate.

Unnurtured

I looked back at the girl who was lost and afraid
Who was scared and alone with nothing to gain
She had given up hope on a life not yet lived
Her spirit was broken she had no more to give
Oh sweet little girl all you craved was
acceptance
For someone to quiet all of the nonsense
The one you looked up to made you feel
worthless
Her words stung like daggers leaving you
hopeless
"You're not enough!"
"No one will love you."
"You deserve nothing!"
She thought maybe it's true
For years she was told this and it tore at her
spirit
As much as she tried she could never unhear it
This poor little girl grew up to believe
She was unworthy and it was better to leave
I looked back at her struggles and what she
endured
I repeat to myself she's not there anymore
The woman who raised me caused me to suffer
The loss of a love between child and mother

To this day I still don't understand
How could she do this, what was her plan
It served no purpose to cause so much grief
It took years of repairing for any relief
No child deserves the pain that was caused
It's not any better now that she's gone
I still find self-love a hard thing to do
But remind myself daily her words were not true
I am loved and enough and can conquer the
world
But that little girl wishes she had heard it from
her.

Soulmate

Raised in turmoil
Seeking acceptance and love
Put a target on your back

You thought attention was love
You thought he was your soulmate
But you learned over time

Soulmates don't manipulate you
Soulmates don't gaslight you
Soulmates don't push you to your wits' end for
their enjoyment

Years of feeling like not enough led you into his
arms
But it took only three to know you didn't belong

It's been years now since you walked away
Years filled with growth and acceptance
From no one but yourself

Time has not only helped you heal
But has given you perspective

You were never taught what true love was

You had little example
You were raised in tolerance not unconditional
love

Then when you stopped searching, there he was
The one who said "I didn't put those holes there,
but I can help you patch them"
The one that says "I love you exactly how you
are"
The one you can't wait to be with.
The one person whose presence is your home.

I didn't know this love.
A love that supported me unconditionally. A
love that pushed me to be better.
A love that no matter what happens is
unwavering.

Each day I spend here, I wish I'd known you
sooner.
Each day I'm glad I know you longer.

That is what makes you my forever Soulmate.

Calm Kitchen

You're the first one here.
You click your key to the right and walk inside.
You hear nothing but the low buzz of the hoods.
You walk around flipping every switch on as if
to say good morning.
The stainless is shining.
You hear the roar of the gas as if the kitchen is
yawning awake from slumber.
This is your happy place.
You can smell the stock that's been simmering
all night.
You feel that bite of cold after you step into the
walk-in.
All of your senses are dancing as you prepare to
start your shift.
The calm before the chaos.
Flavors and techniques define you.
A small rumble from your printer sets your pace.
Soon you will feel hours go by you as if in an
instant and after the rush of the day has subsided
you will close your eyes and remember the quiet
of this moment.
The quiet you enjoy from being the first one
here.
This is your world, Chef.
Let's cook!

Priceless

Hold me tight and hold me close
Right now I need reminding
When everything feels at its worse
That you are right beside me
Touch my face and hold my hand
Tell me what I need to hear
No matter what comes our way
You will still be right here
Things will happen I can't control
Please help me understand
You're the only one who can console
And calm my trembling hands
You softly whisper in my ear
And it pulls me back to life
That I am safe and loved and cared for
Everything will be alright
The weight of fear lifts off my chest
I can finally breathe
I don't think you'll ever know the depth
Or how much to me this means
That I can safely lose control
When my body needs to release
The stress that comes from day to day
Or pain pent up from trauma
The comfort that you bring me

When the shaking is no longer
You never judge my mind's choice
Of letting go of pain
You just hold me near your heart
And remind me once again
I'm right here, I'll never go no matter what the
cause is
You're the one I choose to love
And that to me right there is priceless

Dreams change

Chase your dreams and fight for what
You love no matter what
Are words we hear as little kids all while
growing up
We plan our dreams and make our goals
Filled with endless hope
Not knowing that the world is harsh
Or learning how to cope
The dreams I had at ten years old are nowhere to
be seen
Life had something else in mind I could have
never dreamed
I thought I'd be a teacher helping mold growing
minds
Teaching little ones to read and learning what
was right
A classroom setting with books and charts and
colors all around
A young me never thought that this would not
work out
Until I tried to make it through and struggled
with the course
I lost the drive and joy I had and couldn't find
the source

My plans and dreams seemed to disappear
before my very eyes
Life stepped in and gave to me a very big
surprise
I was meant to be a teacher but not in the way I'd
known
For I was now blessed with a child of my own.
All it took was one look and I found where I
belonged
I'd be his teacher and show him right from
wrong
I will show him love in errors and praise him
when he'd share
I would do everything I could to show him that I
cared
It may not be a classroom but a car themed room
instead
Where he would learn his letters in a story
before bed
He didn't sit in a desk chair when he learned
how to write
But seeing "Mama I luv you" meant I was doing
something right
With everything I taught him he taught me so
much more
This little boy who loved me is what I was
searching for.
He taught me a love that's unconditional and
laughter can cure all

He taught me patience when I thought I might
lose it all
The one lesson that I learned from that sweet
little boy
When all seemed lost back then he would be the
source of my joy

Just like You

I hung up the phone and the panic set in
It was the worst phone call of my life
I never drove so fast on the highway
I was sobbing and screaming and pleading
Please wait! Please wait for me!
I made the three-hour trip in two
As the door opened in front of me the burn of
sanitizer instantly hit my nose
The elevator felt like it was going in slow
motion
I heard the "ding" like symbols in my ears as the
doors opened.
I ran down the hall to your room
You were still here
You waited for me.
I say next to your bed and grabbed your hand
The memory instantly flashed in my mind like
watching a car crash of you squeezing my hand
two days ago
You held so tightly and said "I got my baby girl"
Two days ago you were laughing and joking and
made me promise to change my oil.
The pastor walking in snapped me back to
reality. This can't be real.

Your breath was labored and all I remember is
noise from the preacher. I stopped being able to
understand words.
I kept saying I'm here dad. I made it.
Lost I looked up and almost whispered "he
waited for me"
The pain of watching you was too much for
some and the room once filled with people
dwindled to your girls.
You were still here and I wanted every second.
But as the hours passed we realized you
wouldn't go unless we did.
The doctor told us you were gone minutes after
we left
You were gone
The man I had looked up to my whole life
The man who raised me as his own with no
blood tying us together
The man who taught me everything about what
being a good person was, gone.
I felt every piece of my heart break.
You were selfless and so abundantly full of love.
I wanted to be just like you
I wanted you to be proud of what I became.
More than anything I just wanted you
You held our whole family together and it's
never been the same since that day.
No amount of time has healed the pain of losing
you.

It's been seven years and I still hold you just as
close in my heart as I did back then.
I hope you knew the impact you had on me dad.
I know you knew how much I truly loved you. I
was then and will always be your daddy's little
girl.

Sweet Girl

Freckles on your nose
A dimple by your cheek
Oh sweet little girl
You are just like me

You have a laugh that is contagious
A voice that loves to chat
A smile that is infectious
It's cute how much you love your cat

Your quirky little drawings
And the stories that you tell
Are my pride and joy
And I know you will do well

In no matter what you choose
But what makes me so proud
Is that sweetheart of yours
And when I hear you say out loud

Your hopes and dreams for later
But what you want to do right now
Spend some time with mom
Laughing on the couch

Snacks in hand you snuggle in
With your avocado blanket
You pick our show and turn it up
You know that it's my favorite

You bring me joy
Each time we are together
I love you baby girl
Don't ever forget it

Resentment

You've buried yourself in your mind
There is no escape
You can't see past the fog so you hide from all
the pain
Unbeknownst to you it has stolen all the light
from your eyes
The vile that darkened your soul
now stares you in the face
Your reflection is unknown
You have become what you hate
Blinded by darkness no reason can reach your
ears
You lash out at any mention of correlation
That your demon and you are the same
You are bound to this life as if the chains were
unbreakable
But it's you who hold them in place
You've never known what was stable
Only a world you cannot face
You give in to its will to consume you and it
overtakes
The bond must be broken to let the light in
But fear ties you to this space
She made you feel weak.
She made you feel small.

She took all of your self-worth and beat you
with it
Even the innocent must now feel the wrath that
was meant for her
You feel burning rage when you can't control
those closest in your circle
They must obey your every whim even if it hurts
them.
You crave dominance and let fear be your only
motive
Or the consequence that follows will be
violently explosive
What is maddening is why you choose to be so
cruel
You hated what she did to you but turned out
just like her
That's how the cycle continues
She had no control over how she was raised.
She made her sons pay for the sins of her father
Now you demand the same recourse to make us
pay for the sins of your mother
Is it making sense now?
No longer just a memory but something that
defines you
It holds you captive in its vice unwilling to let
you through

Name your evil and face your fate
Stop before you're numb
There will come a time when it's too late
And the darkness will succumb

Nature

Water is what grounds me
Watching birds fly over a lake
Seeing the sunrise over a pond
Or dancing in the downpour

It calms me and invigorates me
It washes away my stress

The air outside so pure from all the trees
Filled with the smell of damp grass and wet dirt
The perfume of the budding bushes floats
around me
Nothing man-made in sight
That's where I know joy

I can hear the squirrels rustling and cardinals
singing
A small turtle slowly trots by

Peace is everywhere around me and I soak it in
like sunshine

Reaching Your Goal

I have fought the battles
I put in the work
I stood back
And saw all that it took

It didn't come easy
There were times of stress
But I didn't give up
Even when put to the test

They told me to quit
Do something else
But this was my passion
My life that I built

I knew I was good
I knew this was my dream
For all those who doubted
Now look at me

I finally got there
I love what I do
I'm living my life
I'm staying true

If you are in the middle
And feel like losing the fight
Don't give up now
Your dreams are in sight

It's hard and it's terrifying to think
That everything you're trying might break down
and sink
But what if it doesn't
What if it works
You'll get to see all that it's worth

I had my tears
My body felt bruised
But reaching the goal
It's an incredible view

Keep pushing on
Don't quit
I can promise you
It was worth it

Neurodivergent

I knew I was different
But I couldn't explain
My mind was so loud
I was going insane

I had list after list
It needed to be done
But I couldn't move
My body went numb

I'd spend hours and hours
Over every little detail
Getting it perfect
I even skipped meals

I needed quiet and calm
To focus my mind
But my house was chaotic
And I didn't know why

When I would relax
My house was a mess
But super stressed out
I clean in a fit

Does this sound familiar
Ring any bells
How did I miss it
With so many tells

I'm neurodivergent
I wish that I knew
That all of my "quirks"
Were actually clues

Now that I know
Everything is clearer
I'm loving the girl
I see in the mirror

I can finally explain
What I thought all along
My brain is built different
It's not something wrong

Sea of Blue

I know true peace looking into your eyes. It washes over me and the world fades.
I get lost in your sea of blue and hope to never be found.
Your love and passion rush through me like a gust of ocean air.
True and tangible from every angle.
There is no doubt to the depths of your love.
Just like that sea there is no bottom or measure.
No beginning or end.
Time is lost as I am fully encompassed by your soul.
Purest of intentions as clear as the night sky without a single cloud.
Bright as every star that shines, it reflects your truth.
You catch me immersed in that sea of serenity and smile.
In that moment, I see the same peace in you.
I could spend an eternity here.

Autumn Vibes

Crisp cool air and leaves turning red
The scent of cinnamon dancing around
Bonfires and sweaters as the sun sets
Sunday excitement as the coin is tossed
Friends, family and feasts
Apple cider and pumpkin spice
Abundance all around
This is why I love Fall

Owens Poem

I'll hold you and let you cry
The pain you feel is also mine
The joy you felt at two pink lines
Is now your angel in the sky

You'll keep those moments in your heart
You loved him from the very start
How do you handle a grief this large
Robbed of the greatest part

You'll wonder what he sounded like
Asking mommy to hug him tight
Telling him he'll be alright
That's what makes you cry at night

You had plans and hopes and dreams
Now you wonder what it means
Your tears will fall in steady streams
"Why God, why?" your mind will scream

You wanted so bad to be his mother
A loss this deep is like no other
I know that you will always wonder
Even if you have another

If there was a way for you to save
A difference that you could've made
Is there something that you could've given
To give him just one more day

This grief will never disappear
But time will ease the pain that sears
And slowly dry away your tears
Until then I'll be right here

My son has wings just like yours
Everyday I miss him more
I still struggle with that storm
But not the same as I did before

I've been granted peace of mind
Our love forever intertwined
Not alone but by my side
You'll get there too just give it time

Mosaic Heart

Everyday felt like a fight
A battle of wills and I was losing
Tragedy after disaster
I could feel myself drowning
There was no end in sight
No one could survive this
Death and betrayal
I hid in the dark
This could not be it
The losses just got bigger
I was battered and broken
I had nowhere to go
I just buried it deeper
My mind could only take so much
Alone and scared
I finally broke
But breaking was what I needed most
I finally sat with all that happened
I saw the pieces on the floor
I couldn't fix this by myself
I knew I needed help
With a broken heart and open mind
I took the steps I needed
I looked at what was broken
And started picking up the pieces

It hurt a lot the first few times
Those memories were the freshest
But slowly I was able to soften the edges
Time has passed and I see now
The beautiful work of art
Bound by love and forgiveness
My mosaic heart

Daughter's Prayer

I pray you never struggle and
that you always know you're loved
I pray that all your dreams come true and you
chase them with all you got.
I pray you always know that my house is your
home and that you never feel alone.
I pray you shine as bright as your smile is right
now.
I pray you know the strength to get up even
when you're down.
I pray you never stop loving rainbows and the
color blue.
I pray for you everyday baby girl. Oh how I love
you!

Rainbow

Storms have come
Rain so fierce I couldn't see
Lightning flashed
I felt the thunder beneath my feet

But calm set in
Wind became a subtle breeze
The pouring rain subsided
Sunlight poking through the trees

I looked up
I saw the burst of color
A rainbow stretched across the pond
The ultimate reminder

That waiting out the storm
No matter how dark it gets
Will lead you to the beauty
Of what life truly is

Proud

I'm proud of where I am
I love the person I've become
Life did not harshen me
It showed me how to love
It taught me to be humble
And never take for granted
Moments spent with loved ones
You never know when it ends
I finally know what grace is
I learned to forgive
Not only others but myself
This is the life I'm meant to live
I learned to love myself
To admit when I was wrong
Failure doesn't make you weak
Trying makes you strong
I've learned to use my voice
Stand up for what is right
I'm proud to say after everything
I really love my life

Printed in the USA
CPSIA information can be obtained
at www.ICGtesting.com
LVHW011204291024
795100LV00015B/718